Visions of the Vieux Carré

Photography and Text by Kerri McCaffety

PELICAN PUBLISHING COMPANY
Gretna 2013

An 1820s Creole townhouse epitomizes eclectic Vieux Carré style with French antiques, musical instruments, voodoo dolls, and Carnival masks. Above the mantel is a painting commissioned by Napoleon's court celebrating the triumph of freedom in France.

The 1811 Campenel cottage.

"The Vieux Carré combines the sophistication of a large city with the graciousness associated with subtropical climates. The unpretentious elegance and ages-old soul of the Quarter color the rhythms of daily life and allow each of its residents to discover his or her own uniqueness."

—Jon Vaccari

Grotto of Our Lady of Guadeloupe Chapel. Nearing its tricentennial, the French Quarter retains its original city plan, its Latin joie de vivre, *and the religion of its founders—Roman Catholic tradition soaks the air like humidity in the French Quarter. New Orleans is a corner of America where rosary beads hang on a* priedieu.

THANKS
THANKS
THANKS
THANKS
THANKS
THANKS
THANKS
THANKS
THANKS
ALD.

The Williams Residence at the Historic New Orleans Collection.

"Yet beauty lingers here. To say nothing of the picturesque, sometimes you get sight of comfort, sometimes of opulence, through the unlatched wicket in some porte-cochère—red-painted brick pavement, foliage of dark palm or pale banana, marble or granite masonry and blooming parterres . . ."

—George W. Cable, *Old Creole Days, 1879*

Antoine's, the South's oldest restaurant, opened in 1840 and still serves French Creole dishes in an 1831 mansion.

"And what fun to eat all you wanted without having censorious people say you weren't ladylike. And what fun to drink all the champagne you pleased."

—Margaret Mitchell, as Scarlett O'Hara in Gone With the Wind, *1936*

NTOINE'S RESTAURAN

Tujague's opened across the street from the French Market in 1856 to serve the local workers when Levee Street (now Decatur Street) was the center of New Orleans' commerce. The 1827 building occupies the site of an old Spanish armory.

TUJAGUE'S
Decatur
BAR

Charles Etienne Gayarré, one of the first historians of Louisiana, lived at 601 Bourbon Street. Bourbon Street started swinging to the beat of burlesque and glorified vice right after World War II. But among the strip clubs, souvenir shops, and daiquiri bars, fine homes and cafés of a grand era endure.

Rue Bourbon
Bourbon

Built in 1831, this Bourbon Street townhouse has been the address of America's finest French bistro, Galatoire's, since 1905. With Latin fervor and access to the riches of the world, New Orleans developed a taste for the finest of Paris, from absinthe to opera, and extravagant pleasures from cuisine to cocottes.

The pre-eminence of the Quarter's boutiques, filled with Old World treasures and antebellum heirlooms, is rivaled only by the splendor of its hidden rooms and gardens. Often above a store—as they were two hundred years ago—the apartments along Royal are elegant mise-en-scènes *for the drama of French Quarter life.*

Fleur de Paris occupies the first floor of this 1827 building, and above the store, on the second floor, is the salon of Rosemary James' Faulkner House Designs.

St. Louis Cathedral bears the name of the patron saint of Bourbon, France. The first church on the site was destroyed by the hurricane of 1722, and prayers are still offered to Our Lady of Prompt Succor to save the city from destruction every hurricane season.

Interior of the St. Louis Cathedral. The current St. Louis Cathedral was rebuilt in 1852 by the prominent French architect J.N.B. dePouilly and reflects the Greek Revival style of the time.

SANCTUS + SANCTUS + SANCTUS + DOMINUS + DEUS + SABAOTH +

The front arches of the Cabildo. Named for the local Spanish governing body, the Cabildo is the most important building of the Spanish Colonial era. Completed in 1803, it incorporates bits of an earlier 1750s building. In the year of its completion, the Cabildo would see the Spanish, French, and American flags fly over the Place d'Armes.

Café Du Monde serves coffee and beignets in the oldest surviving French Market structure, built in 1813 by the eminent architect-builders Claude Gurlie and Joseph Guillot. Along the river at the edge of Jackson Square, the French Market occupies a trading site established by Indians at the founding of the colony.

WALK

Candles burn for remembered souls at Our Lady of Guadeloupe Chapel, 1826, New Orleans' oldest surviving church.

The weathered front of Preservation Hall, an 1817 townhouse and world-famous traditional jazz venue.

"The wealth of the world is here—unworked gold in the ore. The paradise of the South is here, deserted and half in ruins. I never beheld anything so beautiful and so sad."

—Lafcadio Hearn, Lafcadio Hearn, Life and Letters, *1877*

726

This stoic house on Chartres Street opens onto a French Quarter Eden in back. The first residents of the city, in urban-European style, built houses right at the sidewalk, or banquette, and walled the spaces between. The French Quarter's blocks, still closed from the outside, form an outer wall giving protection from intruders and hurricanes, and hiding the secret majesty within.

A Dauphine Street cottage hides a courtyard and pool behind. While front windows are often rectangular and shuttered, back windows of the same house fan sunlight into an exquisite variety of arches.

The Hermann-Grima House, 1831. Old New Orleans, for all its lavish lifestyle, wore a very humble disguise until American influence crept in during the nineteenth century. Greek Revival and Philadelphia red brick came into vogue by the mid-1800s.

The dainty wrought iron railings of the Chesneau House, circa 1800. Throughout Spanish Colonial times, wrought iron railed balconies were imported from Spain and Mexico or forged in New Orleans.

In the 1850s, the Pontalba buildings changed the face of New Orleans with their bold new cast iron galleries. These verandas could be quite large because of their column-supports, unlike the wood or wrought iron balconies before them that were supported by the building.

Don Bartolome Bosque's house exemplifies Spanish colonial architecture from 1795. The sprawling house surrounds a grand courtyard entered through the carriageway, or porte-cochère. *Bosque, a Spaniard, and his French wife had a daughter, Suzette, a renowned beauty who became the third wife of the American governor, W.C.C. Claiborne. After his death, she married John Randolph Grimes, the lawyer of the pirates Lafitte. The Bosque House occupies the site where the first great fire started in 1788.*

Family crypts. St. Louis Cemetery No. 1 opened on the edge of the French Quarter in 1788, and it was here that above-ground crypts first appeared. Before 1788 the dead were buried on the riverbank or in a graveyard that existed near St. Peter and Burgundy. The tombs of St. Louis Cemetery No. 1 are footprints of history, a chronicle of the region's wars, plagues, economy, and spirituality.

MARIANO RIBAS

A leaning loggia window is a part of the strange jigsaw puzzle that is the Pedesclaux-LeMonnier House, designed c. 1794. In the modern French Quarter renaissance, there is a new admiration for the artful forms of architectural features whose functionality has long passed.

Around 1800 Vincent Rillieux, the great-grandfather of Edgar Degas, commissioned this building that is now Brennan's restaurant. An urban European derivative, the Spanish Colonial house joined the provincial-style cottage on the streets of the growing Vieux Carré, just after the great fire of 1794.

ZONE
MALL

Full of surprises, the Pedesclaux-LeMonnier House is the colossus of a transitional period. French architect Barthélémy Lafon designed the building, begun in 1794 and completed in 1811 by Latour and Laclotte. Called New Orleans' first skyscraper, this building shows strong Spanish Colonial influence with a new height attributed to both American style and advancing technology. The third floor's elliptical salon, with its domed ceiling, must have been a sensation in the nineteenth century. Never before seen in New Orleans, the dome was one of only ten in the United States at the time.

The oversized rooms of the French Quarter allow for audacious blending of styles and periods unified with color.

This 1820 Toulouse Street house shows both a porte-cochère and an entresol. The early Creole townhouse makes the most of its space with two stories—commercial on the first floor and residential above. A walkway or carriageway leads to the courtyard, where an exterior stair leads to upper floors.

514
O'Flaherty's

The Beauregard-Keyes House is another handsome child from the mixed marriage of American and Creole sensibilities. Gabriel's brother, François Correjolles, also an architect, designed the home for Joseph Le Charpentier in 1826.

Hand-blocked wallpaper from 1855 turns the hallway between the Gallier House and service wing into Aramide's garden.

". . . all in her house is dim and beautiful with age. She reclines gracefully upon a dull brocade chaise-lounge, there is the scent of incense about her, and her draperies are arranged in formal folds. She lives in an atmosphere of a bygone and more gracious age."

—William Faulkner, "New Orleans Sketches," 1925

The parlor of Lanaux Mansion. In 1879, architect William Fitzner designed this Esplanade Avenue townhouse for Charles Andrew Johnson, a Connecticut lawyer, who moved to New Orleans in 1840. Johnson died a bachelor in 1896, leaving his house to the woman he loved, Marie Landry Lanaux.

The Gallier House slave quarters are furnished as they would have been in the 1850s.

The Vieux Carré changes and shifts, every day revealing some new magic in the movement of the old. There is no end to the colors and tones of the French Quarter rhapsody. And the music plays on and on.